In the Forest

Shira Evans

NATIONAL GEOGRAPHIC

Washington, D.C.

Table of Contents

CHAPTER 1

What's in the Forest?

Many things in the forest are living. There are plants that grow and change over many years. There are tall trees that started out as small seeds.

Animals live here too. They also grow and change.

The ferns are living too, just like the trees and animals. Living things need food, water and sun to grow.

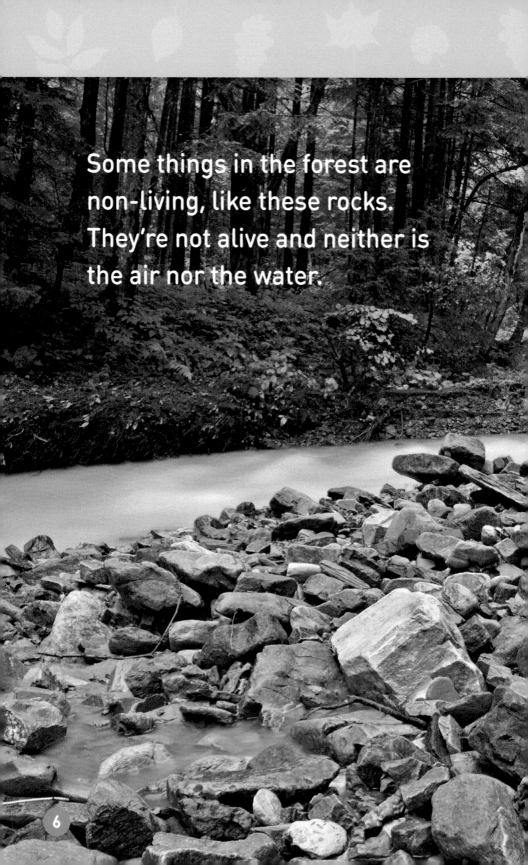

Some things in the forest are non-living, like these rocks. They're not alive and neither is the air nor the water.

Non-living things don't eat or drink, and they don't need air.

YOUR TURN!

Look at the picture. Which things are living and which are non-living?

CHAPTER 2

Changes in the Forest

In the spring, the leaves on the trees are small. They're so small that they don't block the sunlight. The light pours onto the forest floor.

The sunlight helps flowers start
to bloom. New plants grow in
the forest in the spring.

Many animals are born in the spring, such as rabbits, foxes and deer.

These baby animals have
brown fur, which helps them
to blend in with the forest floor
and hide from danger.

During the summer, the forest turns green and is full of leaves. The leaves block the sunlight from reaching the forest floor.

Fruits, berries and nuts begin to grow in the summer. They will soon be ready to eat.

In the summer, the forest is warm and more fruit grows.

Animals eat the ripe
fruits and berries.
The chatter of
busy animals fills
the air.

In the autumn, the days get shorter and colder. There is less sunlight, and the leaves start to lose their green colour.

Soon the leaves will drop.
In the autumn, leaves
cover the forest floor.

Chipmunks and squirrels gather acorns in the autumn. They hide the nuts under leaves or in nests in the trees.

Animals work hard in the autumn. They save the nuts to eat later.

Winter days are short and the sun is low in the sky. The animals slow down and the forest looks empty.

The forest is quiet in the winter.
It's cold and still.

Many animals hibernate in the winter. They slow down their heartbeats and sleep for a long time.

In the winter, some animals
stay warm in their dens.
Others sleep in caves.

YOUR TURN!

Point to each picture. Say what season it shows.

> spring
> summer
> autumn
> winter

CHAPTER 3

Helping the Forest

This beaver is building a wall out of logs. It has to push the heavy logs into the water. Each log helps it build a bigger and bigger wall.

The wall makes a dam.
Beavers build dams to
keep their homes safe.

A dam also stops the river water from flowing. When the water doesn't flow, it forms a pond. The water level rises.

When the water level rises,
more plants can grow.
The beavers' dam helps
these new plants.

A bird called a cardinal lands on a bush in the forest. The bush has bright red berries. The berries are food for the bird.

Soon the bird flies away.
It will land in a new part
of the forest.

As the cardinal flies, it drops the seeds from the berries throughout the forest. The seeds scatter on the forest floor.

New bushes grow where the cardinal drops the seeds. The bird helps the forest to grow.

Plants help
animals in the
forest, too! Some
trees hang low over
streams and ponds.
They shade the water
from the hot sun.

The fish in the stream need cool water. But the sun is hot. The trees shade the water. That helps the water stay cool.

Fungi are not plants or animals, but they can help the forest, too. Some fungi grow on trees and feed on things that have died. The fungi turn dead leaves and wood into soil.

Plants use the new soil to grow. The fungi help the forest.

YOUR TURN!

Animals and plants help the forest. What can people do to help the forest? Look at the pictures for ideas.

1

CHAPTER 4

Life in the Forest

Some animals make homes up high in forest trees. Others live down low.

A bird lives in a nest high in
a tree. A fox builds a den low
on the ground.

Although there are different types of plants and animals in the forest, they need one another to grow.

Animals and plants
need different things.
But they all live together
in the forest.

YOUR TURN!

Some of the forests in this book are deciduous forests. That means they are in a place with both warm and cool weather, and the trees change throughout each season. Here's where deciduous forests are found around the world. Find where you live. Are there deciduous forests near you?

EQUATOR

PACIFIC OCEAN

NORTH AMERICA

SOUTH AMERICA

ATLANTIC OCEAN

AFRICA

EUROPE

ARCTIC OCEAN

A S I A

INDIAN OCEAN

AUSTRALIA

PACIFIC OCEAN

ANTARCTICA

Where deciduous forests are found

Published by Collins
An imprint of HarperCollins*Publishers*
The News Building
1 London Bridge Street
London
SE1 9GF

HarperCollinsPublishers
1st Floor, Watermarque Building
Ringsend Road
Dublin 4, Ireland

Browse the complete Collins catalogue at
www.collins.co.uk

In association with National Geographic Partners, LLC

NATIONAL GEOGRAPHIC and the Yellow Border Design are trademarks of the National Geographic Society, used under license.

Second edition 2018
First published 2016

ISBN 978-0-00-831720-1

10 9 8 7 6 5

Printed and bound in the UK by Pureprint

If you would like to comment on any aspect of this book, please contact us at the above address or online.
natgeokidsbooks.co.uk
cseducation@harpercollins.co.uk

Since 1888, the National Geographic Society has funded more than 12,000 research, exploration, and preservation projects around the world. The Society receives funds from National Geographic Partners, LLC, funded in part by your purchase. A portion of the proceeds from this book supports this vital work. To learn more, visit http://natgeo.com/info.

Illustration Credits

Cover, David Courtenay/Getty Images; Top border (throughout), Undina/Shutterstock; 1 (CTR), Johnny Johnson/Getty Images; 2 Erik Mandre/Shutterstock; 3 (LO), andamanec/Shutterstock; 4 (LO), imagenavi/Getty Images; 5 (CTR), Bendiks Westerink/Minden Pictures; 6-7 (CTR), VIDOK/Getty Images; 8-9 (CTR), Danita Delimont/Getty Images; 9 (CTR), Mike Truchon/Shutterstock; 10-11 (UP), Anneka/Shutterstock; 12 (LE), Don Johnston/Getty Images; 12 (UP), Brian Gordon Green/Getty Images; 13 (UP), Christina Ascani; 14-15 (UP), Michael Skelton/Getty Images; 15 (CTR), BoxerX/Shutterstock; 16 (UP), Brian E. Kushner/Getty Images; 16 (LO), imageBROKER/Alamy; 17 (CTR), Jack Chapman/Minden Pictures; 18-19 (CTR), Chris Hepburn/Getty Images; 20 (CTR), Philippe Clement/Minden Pictures; 20 (UP), Alina Morozova/Getty Images; 21 (CTR), jurra8/Shutterstock; 22-23 (CTR), Franz Pritz/Getty Images; 24 (UP), Danny Green/Minden Pictures; 25 (LO), Juniors Bildarchiv/Alamy; 26 (LO), Cornelia Doerr/Getty Images; 26 (CTR), Dennis van de Water/Shutterstock; 27 (UP), Michael Skelton/Getty Images; 27 (LO), Konrad Wothe/LOOK-foto/Getty Images; 28 (LO), Donald M. Jones/Getty Images; 29 (UP), Chase Dekker Wild-Life Images/Getty Images; 30-31 (CTR), David Hosking/Minden Pictures; 32 (CTR), B&S Draker/Minden Pictures; 33 (UP), Alan Murphy/Minden Pictures; 34-35 (CTR), Danita Delimont/Getty Images; 36 (CTR), Ursula Sander/Getty Images; 37 (LO), Franco Banfi/Getty Images; 38 (CTR), Eric Gibcus/Minden Pictures; 39 (UP), Michael P Gadomski/Getty Images; 39 (LO), Tetsuya Tanooka/Aflo/Getty Images; 40 (CTR), Tetra Images - Mike Kemp/Getty Images; 41 (UP), Hero Images/Getty Images; 41 (LO), KidStock/Blend Images/Getty Images; 42 (CTR), Harri Taavetti/Minden Pictures; 43 (UP RT), Jim Brandenburg/Minden Pictures; 43 (CTR), Ronald Stiefelhagen/ NiS/Getty Images; 44 (CTR LE), Dreamstime.com; 44 (CTR RT), kamnuan/Shutterstock; 44 (CTR), Sari ONeal/Shutterstock; 44 (LO), oksana2010/Shutterstock; 45 (CTR RT), Eric Isselee/Shutterstock; 45 (UP), Sebastian Kennerknecht/Minden Pictures; 47 (CTR), NG Maps

Paper from responsible sources